The Wooden Prince
for Solo Piano
Op. 13

The composer's original piano transcription
of his complete music for Béla Balázs'
dance-play in one act

Béla Bartók

DOVER PUBLICATIONS, INC.
Mineola, New York

Bibliographical Note

This Dover edition, first published in 2001, is an unabridged republication of *Der holzgeschnitzte Prinz / Tanzspiel in einem Akt von Béla Balázs / Musik von Béla Bartók / Op. 13 / Piano Solo,* originally published by Universal-Edition, Vienna, 1921. Lists of credits, contents, and instrumentation, as well as a prefatory note and story synopsis, are newly added.
We are indebted to Stanley Appelbaum for biographical information about Béla Balázs included in the note "Bartók and Balázs"; and to The Sibley Music Library, Eastman School of Music, for the loan of this rare score for republication.

International Standard Book Number: 0-486-41679-8

Manufactured in the United States of America
Dover Publications, Inc., 31 East 2nd Street, Mineola, N.Y. 11501

To Egisto Tango

THE WOODEN PRINCE
A dance-play in one act

Op. 13

Music by | Play by
Béla Bartók | **Béla Balázs**

●

ORIGINAL FULL-LENGTH SCORE

• Composed 1914–16 • Orchestrated 1916–17 • Published 1924
• Piano transcription of the full score by the composer, published 1921
• First performance: 12 May 1917 / Opera, Budapest; Egisto Tango conducting

The first concert version, a little Suite with a new ending, consists of Dances II, III and V;
a subsequent five-part version restored the prelude and postlude and rearranged the order of dances.

●

CHARACTERS AND ELEMENTS OF THE PLAY

The prince, the princess, the fairy, the wooden prince, the forest, the stream

STAGE SETTING

A grotesque, primitive scene with a large rock center stage. Front left, a hill encircled by a stream and surmounted by a tiny castle without a front wall; within the castle, a tiny room with a chair and spinning wheel before a small window. A narrow path leads from castle to stream, then over a tree-bridge into a forest on the left. The trees stand in four even rows. A second path runs across stage to a hill in the right rear, topped by a tiny castle with a front wall.

Bartók and Balázs

About 1911, faced with public and publisher disinterest in his new music, Béla Bartók, then 30 years old, increasingly devoted his attention to ethnomusicology through field investigations of the folk music of Hungary, Bulgaria, Romania, Slovakia, and North Africa. Bartók's research profoundly shaped his growth as a composer, first in early piano pieces and songs based on folk song, and in the Piano Suite (1916) and Second String Quartet (1915–17), both influenced by his immersion in Arab music.

This fundamental shaping force was particularly evident in the substance and formation of the dance-play *The Wooden Prince* (1914–16), both in its modal melodic lines and in elements of the story itself: the mixture of naive fairy tale and mystic natural forces, of love-sacrifice, in its depiction of good and evil forces, and especially in its focus on the conflict of perception and reality.

The scenario of the dance-play (some call it a ballet) *A fából faragott királyfi*—literally, "The Prince Carved Out of Wood"—was written by the outstanding Hungarian playwright, poet, novelist, literary critic, film theorist, and filmmaker Béla Balázs (nom de plume of Herbert Bauer). At a teachers' college in Budapest, Balázs was the roommate of the future great composer and music educator Zoltán Kodály. These two met Bartók in 1905, and all three went on field trips together to collect folk music. Thus it was Balász who worked with Bartók in the 1910 publication of his piano cycle *For Children,* translating Slovakian song texts into Hungarian; who wrote the play (dedicated to Kodály and Bartók, 1910) that became Bartók's opera *Bluebeard's Castle;* and who, in 1914, wrote the new piece *The Wooden Prince* specifically for Bartók, and served as stage director for its world premiere in 1917.

SYNOPSIS

As the curtain rises, the fairy is seen standing at the foot of a hill, the princess sitting in the woods. The princess moves about, making playful gestures.

DANCE I (pp. 8–12): *"Dance of the princess in the forest."* The fairy moves, drawing strange wide bows with her arms over the surroundings, then walks slowly into the forest. The princess, wholly undisturbed, goes on dancing. The door of the second little castle opens and the prince appears. The fairy repeatedly bids the princess to return to her castle, but the young girl mirthfully opposes the command, still dancing to and fro. The fairy finally succeeds as the princess leaves, crosses the narrow tree-bridge, and disappears.

Leaving his castle, the prince encounters the fairy but turns away. As the princess now enters *her* castle, the prince catches sight of her and instantly falls in love, hardly able to contain himself. Unaware of her admirer, the princess enters a tiny room where she begins work at her spinning wheel. Pondering his next move, the smitten prince is determined to go to his beloved. Running toward her castle, he is suddenly thwarted as the fairy enchants the forest in his path.

DANCE II (pp. 14–21): *"Dance of the trees."* The prince is terrified as the forest is brought to life. Gathering up his courage, the prince strides toward the enchanted forest, successfully fighting his way through. The forest gradually calms down.

Pursuing his plan, the prince approaches the tree-bridge, but the fairy blocks him yet again, now enchanting the waters of the stream.

DANCE III (pp. 22–28): *"Dance of the waves."* The stream overflows, lifting the bridge, blocking the prince. Each disheartened retreat and renewed assault is mirrored by a momentary calming, then quickening, of the waves as they block his way. In despair, the prince returns to the forest where he considers his next move.

Pursuing a new idea to attract the princess's attention (p. 28), the prince slips his cloak around his walking staff, steps up on a rock, then lifts his adorned staff high in the air. But his anxiety only increases as the princess, absorbed in her weaving, pays scant attention to the odd distraction. Now fastening his *crown* to the staff and repeating his efforts (p. 33), the poor prince has no better success; the object of his love sees it all but shows not the least interest. "Maybe *this* will do it," he thinks, as he cuts his golden locks and fastens *them* to his staff (p. 34). Success! Charmed by the sight of this new toy, the princess races merrily down from her castle (pp. 35–36).

The prince now reveals himself but the princess flees from his embrace. Entering into the game, the fairy brings the adorned staff to life. It is a contest (pp. 38–40): the princess seeks the wooden prince . . . the true prince intervenes . . . the princess angrily evades the prince. She succeeds at last, beginning a lengthy dance with the doll.

DANCE IV (pp. 40–49): *"Dance of the princess with the wooden doll."* The princess and her wooden prince exit at last, still dancing, leaving the real prince behind in the greatest despair. In his grief he lies down and falls asleep. The fairy steps out of the forest, goes to him, and gently comforts him.

At her command, all things around her are given life and now, in rendering homage to the prince, dance before him (pp. 52–54). From one flower's center, then another, the fairy takes curly golden hair, then a crown, to adorn his head; from yet another, a cloak of flowers to lay around his shoulders. There is a great apotheosis (pp. 54–55) as all of nature pays him homage—the trees, the waters, the flowers. In triumph, radiance and splendor, the fairy leads the prince to the hill: "Here you will be king over everything!"

The scene is interrupted by the abrupt arrival of the princess and her wooden prince (pp. 55–56), but everything about the doll is in disarray: his wig, his cloak, his crown.

DANCE V (pp. 56–58): *"The princess in her endeavor to make him dance, pulls and pushes the wooden prince about."* Her anger only worsens the situation: his dance movements deteriorate. Soon she grows to hate him. She pushes him away. He falls to the floor. Then she sees the real prince in all his radiant splendor.

DANCE VI (pp. 59–60): *"With her most fascinating smiles, the princess tries to persuade the prince to her side to dance with her."* But the prince touches his heart, then makes a disavowing gesture and turns away from her.

DANCE VII (pp. 62–65): *"Quite alarmed, the princess hurries forward to him, yet the forest keeps her from him."* Every effort to overcome these obstacles is hopeless. She turns away, now stumbling over the discarded wooden prince; she kicks him angrily. Now in utter despair, the princess throws off her crown and cloak, finally cutting off her hair. Then she sits down, burying her face in her hands.

Meanwhile, the prince has reentered the scene (pp. 66–end). Seeing the princess in pain, he tries to console her. She is ashamed of her bareness, yet the prince persists, finally embracing her with great tenderness. Little by little, the enchanted objects that surround them regain their original shapes and their original places as the curtain falls.

END

The Wooden Prince
for Solo Piano
Op. 13

INSTRUMENTATION

4 Flutes [Flauti, Fl.]
    Fls. 3/4 double Piccolo [Ottavini, Ott.]

4 Oboes [Oboi, Ob.]
    Obs. 3/4 double English Horn [Corni inglesi, Cor. ing.]

2 Saxophones [Saxofoni, Sax.]
    (E♭ Alto; B♭ Tenor doubles E♭ Baritone)

4 Clarinets in A & B♭ [Clarinetti, Clar (La, Si♭)]
    Clar. 3 doubles E♭ Clarinet
    Clar. 4 doubles Bass Clarinet in A & B♭ [Clarinetto Basso, Cl. b. (La, Si♭)]

4 Bassoons [Fagotti, Fag.]
    Fag. 3/4 double Contrabassoon [Contrafagotti, Cfag.]

4 Horns in F [Corno/i, Cor. (Fa)]
4 Trompets in B♭ [Tromba/e), Tr., Tr.-e (Si♭)]
2 Cornets in B♭ [Cornette a pistoni, Cnt., Ct., Pist. (Si♭)]
3 Trombones [Tromboni, Tr.-ni.]
Tuba [Tuba bassa]

Timpani [Timpani, Timp.]

Percussion

Bass Drum [Gran Cassa, G.C.]	Snare Drum [Tamburo piccolo, Tam. picc.]
Bells [Campanelli, Camp.]	Tam-tam [Tamtam, Tt.]
Castanets [Castagnetti, Cast.]	Triangle [Triangolo, Triang.]
Cymbals [Piatti, Ptti.]	Xylophone[Xilofono, Xyl.]

Celesta [Celesta, Cel.]
2 Harps [Arpa/e, Arp.]

Violins I, II [Violino/i, Viol.]
Violas [Viole, Vle., Ve.]
Cellos [Violoncelli, Vc.]
Basses [Contrabassi, Cb.]

Other abbreviations in the piano score:
arco = bowed / col legno = played with the wood of the bow
Cord(e) = string instruments / c. sord., con sordino = muted
Flageolet, Flag. = harmonics / Harmonie, Harm. = wind instruments
pizzicato, pizz. = plucked strings / tremolo, trem. = rapid pitch alternation

DER HOLZGESCHNITZTE PRINZ.

Tanzspiel in einem Akt.

A fából faragott királyfi.   The wooden prince.

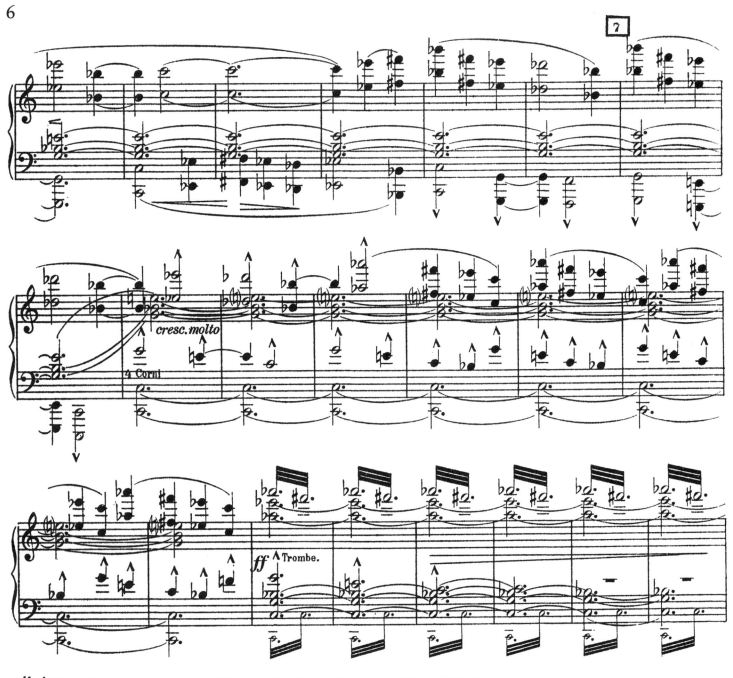

7

Vorhang: *(Die Fee steht links am Fuße des Hügels, die Prinzessin sitzt im Walde.)*
Függöny: *(A tündér a domb bal oldalán áll, a királykisasszony az erdőben ül.)*
Curtain: *(The fairy is seen standing on the left at the foot of the hill, the princess sitting in the wood.)*

8 (♩ = 144)

ritardando – – – – – – –

(*Die Prinzessin rührt sich, macht spielerische Bewegungen.*)
(*A királykisasszony játékos mozdulatai.*)
(*The princess moves, making playful gestures.*)

I. Tanz. Tanz der Prinzessin im Walde.
I. Tánc. A királykisasszony tánca az erdőben.
I. Dance. Dance of the princess in the forest.

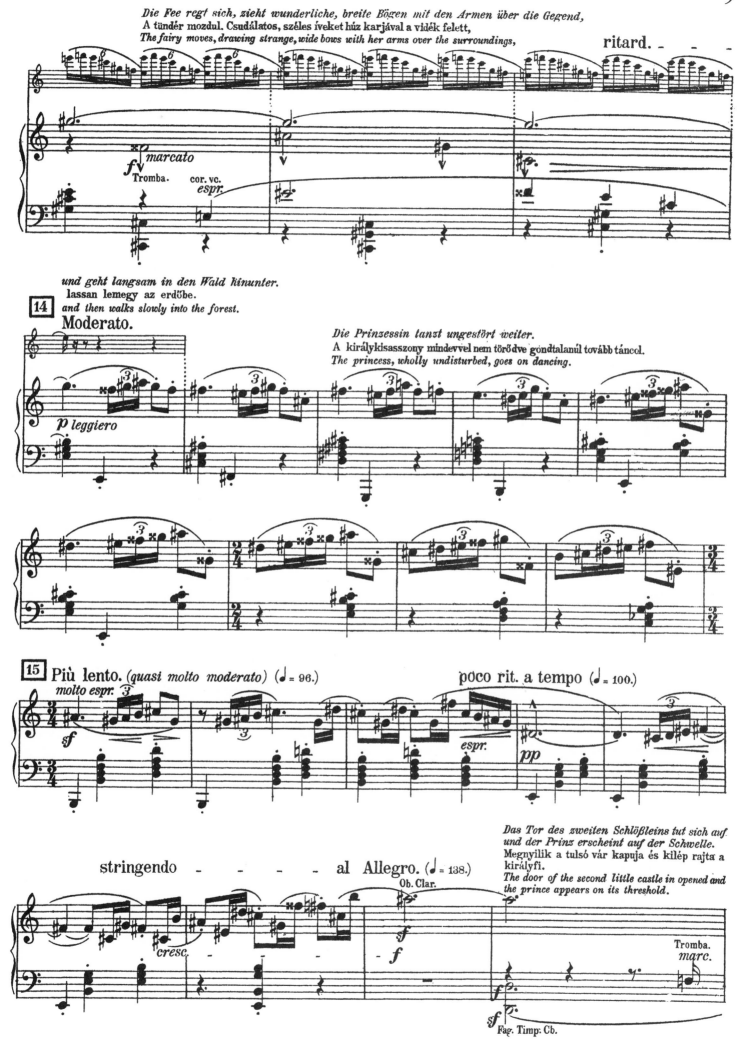

Die Fee regt sich, zieht wunderliche, breite Bögen mit den Armen über die Gegend,
A tündér mozdul. Csudálatos, széles íveket húz karjával a vidék felett,
The fairy moves, drawing strange, wide bows with her arms over the surroundings,

ritard.

f marcato
Tromba.
cor. vc.
espr.

und geht langsam in den Wald hinunter.
lassan lemegy az erdőbe.
14
and then walks slowly into the forest.
Moderato.

Die Prinzessin tanzt ungestört weiter.
A királykisasszony mindevvel nem törődve gondtalanúl tovább táncol.
The princess, wholly undisturbed, goes on dancing.

p leggiero

15 Più lento. (quasi molto moderato) (♩ = 96.)
molto espr.
sf

poco rit. a tempo (♩ = 100.)
espr.
pp

Das Tor des zweiten Schlößleins tut sich auf
und der Prinz erscheint auf der Schwelle.
Megnyílik a túlsó vár kapuja és kilép rajta a
királyfi.
The door of the second little castle in opened and
the prince appears on its threshold.

stringendo _ _ _ _ al Allegro. (♩ = 138.)
Ob. Clar.

cresc.
sf
f

Tromba.
marc.

sf
Fag. Timp. Cb.

Die Fee gebietet mit energischen Bewegungen Rükkehr dem Prinzeßchen. (6 Bewegungen.)
A tündér az erdőben az őt körültáncoló királykisasszonyt fölparancsolja a várába.(6 mozdulat.)
The fairy, with energetic gestures, bids the princess to return to her castle. (6 movements.)

Die Prinzessin sträubt sich übermütig gegen den Befehl, tanzt hin und her.
A királykisasszony pajkosan ellenszegül a parancsnak, el-eltáncol, pajzánkodik.
The princess mirthfully opposes the command, still dancing to and fro.

Più allegro. ($\bullet$ = 176.)

Meno mosso. ($\bullet$ = 152.)

Die Fee wiederholt die befehlenden Gesten,
A tündér megismétli parancsát.
The fairy repeats the commanding gestures.

Die Prinzessin setzt das übermütige Spiel fort,
A királykisasszony megismétli előbbi játékát,
The princess continues her play with unrestrained mirth,

Più allegro. (♩= 176.)

doch gelingt es endlich der Fee, sie hinauf
végre mégis sikerül a tündérnek őt a vár fe-
but the fairy finally succeeds in driving her uphill.

zu treiben. Die Prinzessin schreitet über den Steg und
lé hajtani; áthalad a hidon
The princess crosses the narrow bridge (tree-bridge) and

Ende des I. Tanzes.
I. tánc vége.
End of the I. dance.
verschwindet.
felfelé haladtán eltünik szemünk elől.
disappears.

Vivacissimo. (♩ = 76 -70)

Der Prinz macht sich auf den Weg. Sein Gang ist zögernd, er schaut nach rechts u. links. Währenddessen kehrt die Fee um und kommt durch den Wald dem Prin-
A királyfi a tulsó vár kapujából lassan elindul, eleinte keveset haladva, a tündér közben visszafordúl és az erdőn át a királyfi felé tart.
The prince starts on his way. In his slow, lingering gait he looks to left and right. Meanwhile the fairy turns round and, coming through the forest, meets the prince.

19 **Andante.** (♩ = 100)

Der Prinz erblickt sie, wendet sich ab und schlägt eine andere Richtung ein.
A királyfi meglátja a tündért, elfordul, irányt változtat; lefelé haladása határozottabbá válik.
The prince, espying her, turns from her and walks away in another direction.

a tempo (♩ = 112)

Die Prinzessin wird, als sie ihr Schloß betreten will, sichtbar.
A királykisasszony, mielőtt várába beérne, ismét láthatóvá lesz.
The princess is seen as she enters her castle.

20 **accel.**

Der Prinz erblickt sie, wird sofort von Liebe zu ihr erfaßt, kann sich vor Aufregung kaum halten. Die Prinzessin merkt von all
A királyfi, amint a színpad jobb szélére ért, felnéz a dombra és meglátja a királykisasszonyt, egyszeribe beleszeret, előre fut, jobbra fut, balra fut,
The prince, catching sight of her, falls in love with her and is hardly able to restrain his excited feelings. All the foregoing events do not come to the

dem nichts und verschwindet in ihrem Schloß. Sie tritt in ihr Stübchen, setzt sich ans Spinnrad und spinnt.
azt se tudja hová fusson. De a királykisasszony, anélkül hogy a királyfit észrevette volna, eltünik vára kapujában.
notice of the princess, who disappears within her castle. She enters her tiny room and, after sitting down at her spinning-wheel, begins to spin.

Der Prinz: „Ich liebe sie!"
A királyfi szerelmes mozdulata.
The prince: "I love her!"

Er setzt sich und sinnt nach, was zu tun wäre.
A királyfi leül, fájdalmasan töpreng, mitévő legyen.
He sits down, pensive as to what to undertake next.

Er springt auf.
Felugrik.
Suddenly he jumps up:

„Ich gehe einfach zu ihr hinauf.". Und schon läuft er dem Walde zu.
„Felmegyek hozzá, ez a legegyszerűbb"...és már fut is az erdő felé.
"I simply shall go up to her!"__ and runs across to the forest.

Allegro. ($\dot\circ$=152)

Cord.
mf
cresc.

Doch wie er hingelangt, hebt
22 *Amint már szinte az erdőhöz*
But in reaching it, the fairy raises

f

Corni.

die Fee die Arme und verzaubert den Wald (3 Gesten).
ért, a tündér bűvös köröket rajzol karjaival (3 mozdulat).
her arms and enchants the forest (3 gestures).

Tromba.
marcato

Più vivo. ($\dot\circ$=160)

ff

II.Tanz.(Tanz der Bäume). Der
Wald belebt sich.

II. tánc. Az erdő megmozdul (ele-
inte bizonytalan, nem táncszerű
mozdulatok.)
II. Dance.(Dance of the trees). The forest now being brought to life, the prince gazes

Der Prinz schaut starr vor Schrecken
A királyfi kétszer is _ _ _ _ _ _ _ _ _ *visszahököl, majd kővé*
_ _ _ _ _ _ _ _ _ *full of terror*

23
Assai moderato. ($\dot\circ$=72)
mp
Clar. Ob.
Clar.
p

Cb. con sord.
pizz.

ppp

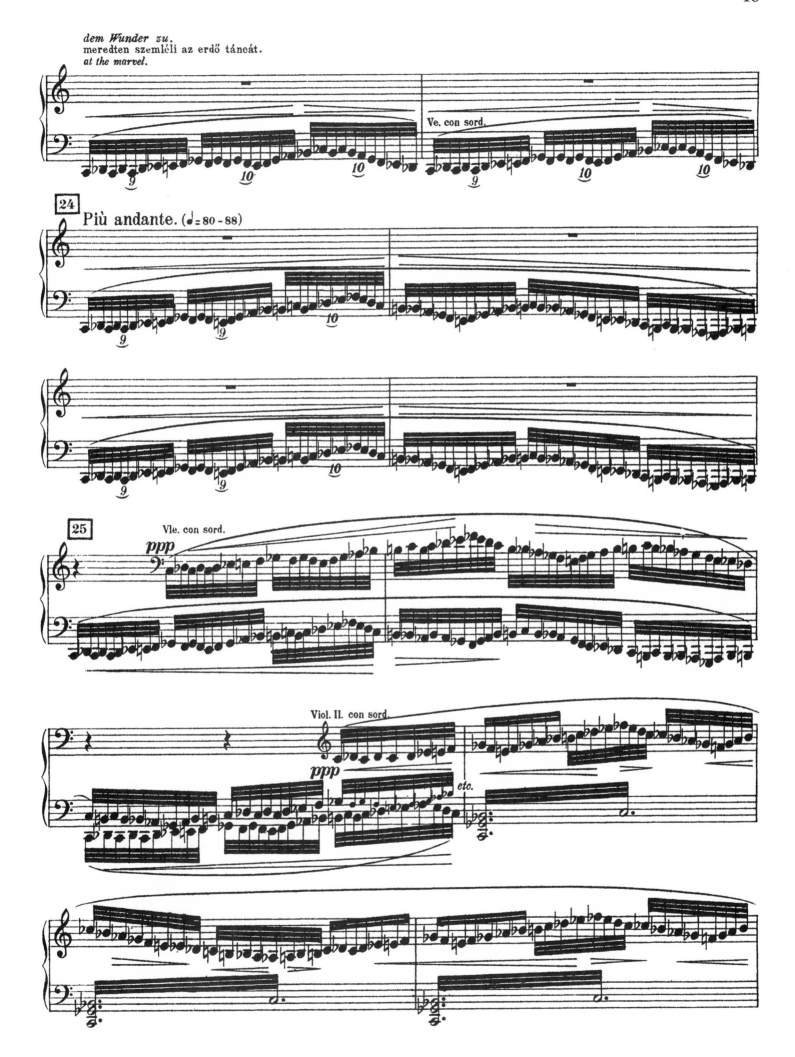

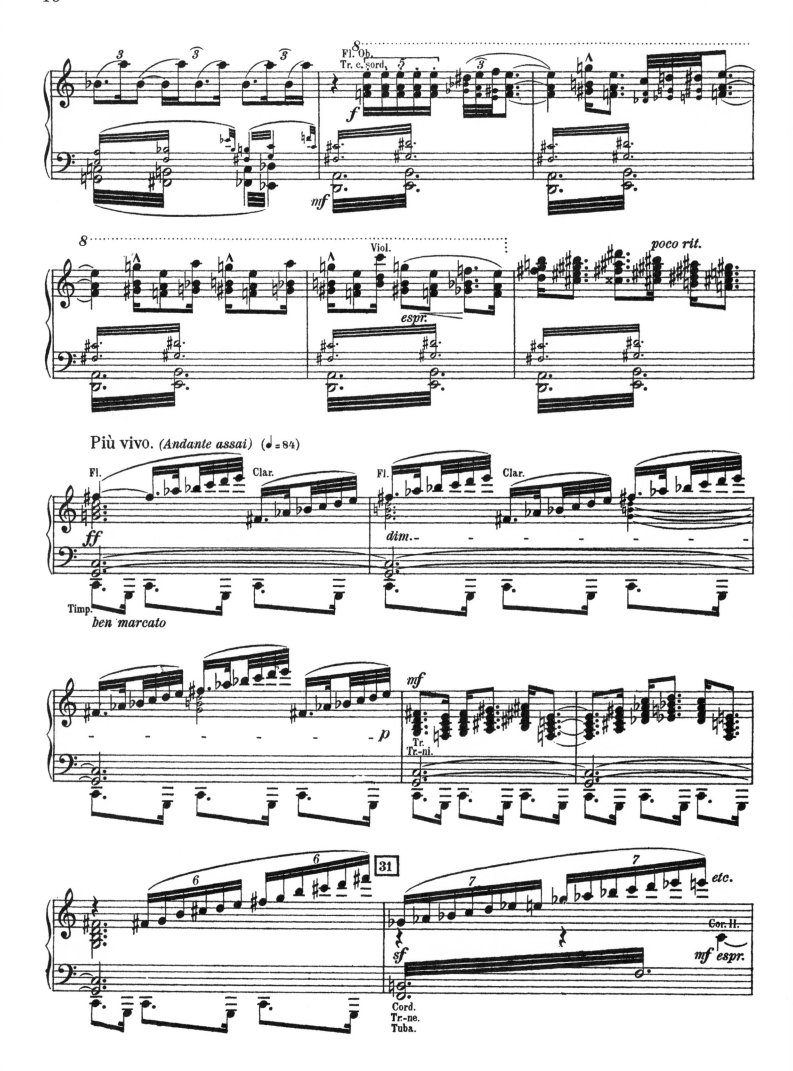

Der Prinz geht entschlossen auf den Wald los. (Kampf)
A királyfi hirtelen nekimegy az erdőnek (küzdelemtánc).
Energetically the prince walks towards the forest and a fight ensues.

Es gelingt ihm, sich durchzuringen;
A királyfinak sikerült átjutnia az erdőn,
He succeeds in getting through;

der Wald beruhigt sich allmählich.
mely lassanként lecsendesedik.
the forest calms down by degrees.

III.Tanz. (Wellentanz) der Bach steigt aus seinem Bette und hebt den Steg hoch. Der Prinz versucht verschiedenemal über die Wel-
III.Tánz. A patak fölemelkedik medrében és fölemeli a hidat. A királyfi visszahököl, nézi a játékot; próbálna átmenni,
III.Dance.(Dance of the waves). The stream rises beyond its bed and lifts the bridge. The prince repeatedly tries to cross over the bridge,

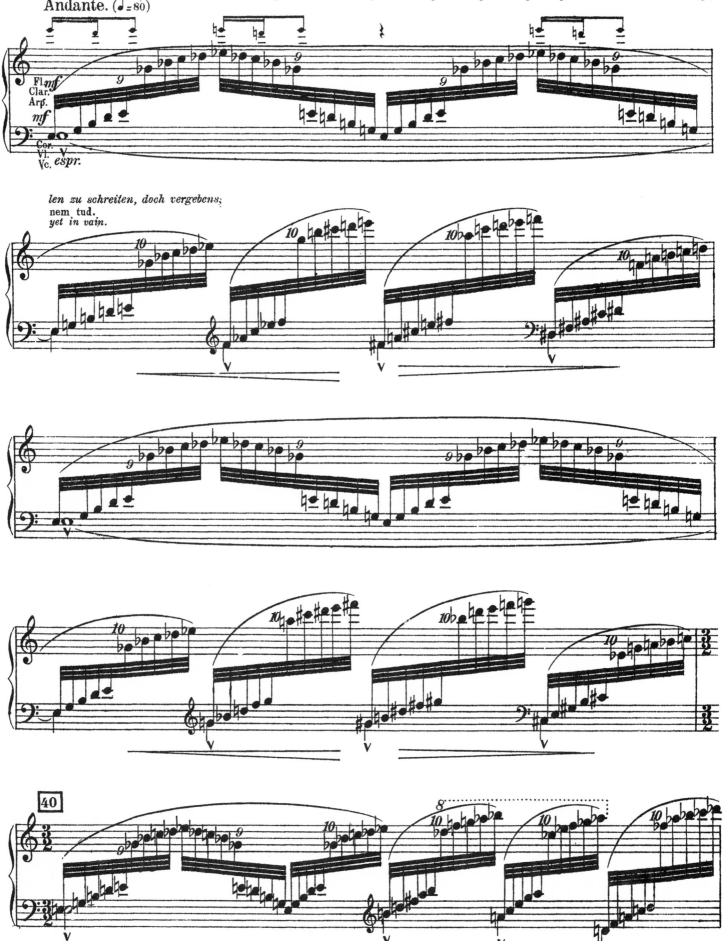

len zu schreiten, doch vergebens;
nem tud.
yet in vain.

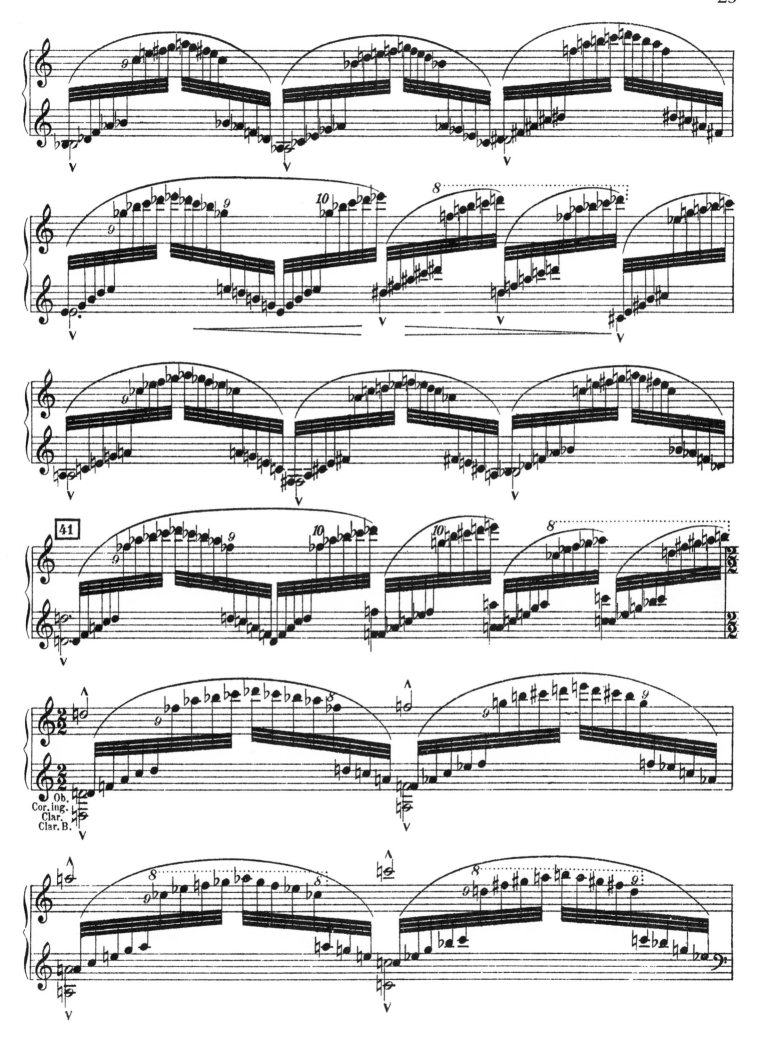

er kehrt mutlos zurück, worauf sich die Heftigkeit des Wellentanzes legt.
A királyfi csüggedten visszaballag; a hullámok szinte lecsendesednek.
He turns back, fully disheartened, whereat the impetuosity of the wave-dance becomes milder.

Sobald der Prinz dessen gewahr wird, erneuert er seinen Versuch, worauf der Wellentanz sofort wieder heftig einsetzt.
A királyfi ujra nekimegy a pataknak, mire a hullámzás ujra megkezdődik.
As soon as the prince becomes aware of this he renews his attempts, yet at this the wave-dance starts with new force.

Der Prinz sieht das Vergebliche seiner Bemühungen ein; (die Wellen beruhigen sich allmählich,) voller Verzweiflung geht er wieder
A királyfi nem tud átjutni a patakon, - (a patak megnyugszik,) - visszakullog az erdő tulsó szélére,
The prince perceives the fruitlessness of his endeavours. (the waves are calming down successively) full of despair the prince walks back through
the forest,

durch den Wald zurück,

setzt sich, und sinnt nach.
leül, gondolkozik:
sits down, thoughtfully.

Er hat eine Idee.
ötlete támad:
An idea enters his mind.

Er nimmt seinen Stab, und richtet ihn her, um seinen Mantel darauf hängen zu können.
nekiül, hogy botját kikészitse és ráakassza palástját.
He takes up his staff, prepares it so that he may put his cloak on it.

53 **Meno allegro.** (σ = 116-126)

32

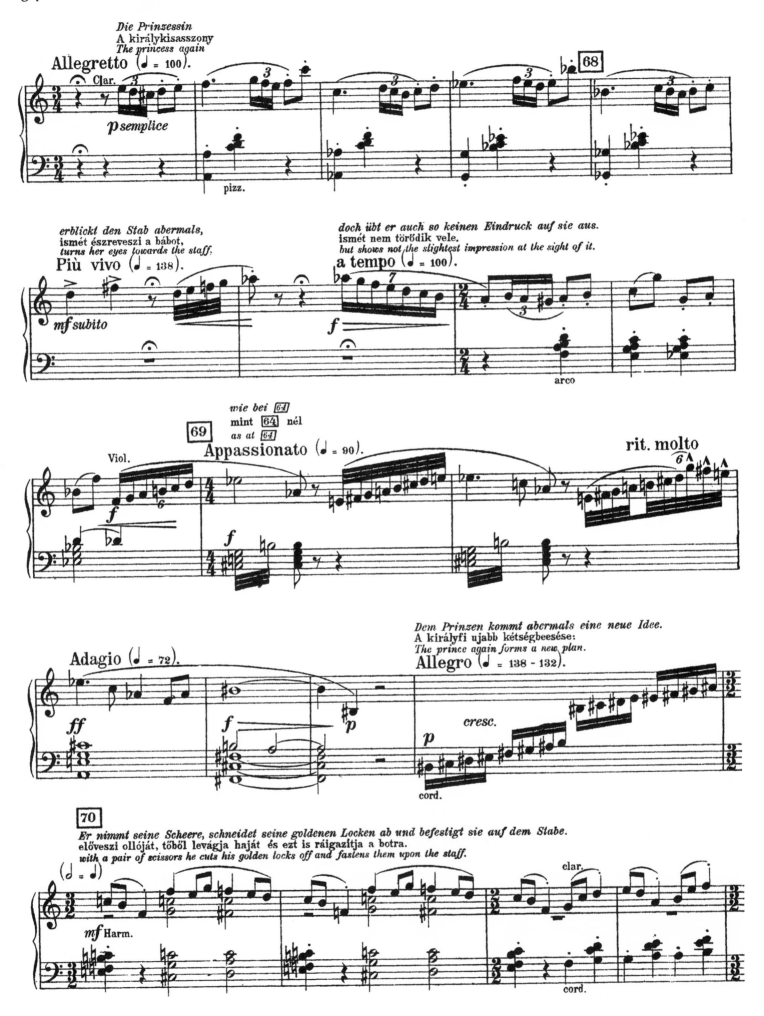

Er hält den Stab hoch empor.
A királyfi ismét felmutatja a bábot.
He raises the staff high up.

Sostenuto (♩ = 76).

Die Prinzessin bemerkt den goldlockigen Stab,
A királykisasszony észreveszi a bábot;
The princess notices the staff with the golden locks,

Allegretto (♩ = 120).

er gefällt ihr, sie will ihn haben, und kommt auch schon froh-
a báb megtetszik neki,- indul is már le a váracskájából.
the sight pleases her, and with the desire take possession of it, comes

Allegro (♩. = 80).

lockend aus ihrem Schlößchen zum schöner Spielzeug herab.
jubilating down from her little castle to the pretty toy.

Die Prinzessin ist unten ange-
langt. Der Prinz tritt hinter dem
Stabe hervor und breitet seine
Arme nach ihr aus.
A királykisasszony leér; a király-
fi kilép a földbe szúrt báb mögül
és kitárja karját,
The princess has arrived. The
prince comes from behind the staff
and stretches his arms wide to
embrace her.

Doch sie weicht erschaudernd vor
dem schmucklosen Jünglinge zurück.
Verfolgungsspiel.
de a királykisasszony undorodva me-
nekül előle.
But the princess flees trembling from the
austere youth.(Cat and mouse play)

Vivace. ($\bullet$ = 120.)

87

Più mosso. ($\bullet$ = 134.)

88

Die Prinzessin hat die Holzpuppe erreicht: IV. Tanz. (Tanz der Prin-
A királykisasszony elérte a bábot; táncra perdül vele. (IV. tánc.)
The princess finally reaches the wooden doll. IV. Dance. (Dance of the princess
with wooden doll.)

Allegro. ($\bullet$ = 123.)

zessin mit der Holzpuppe.)

89

meno f

cresc.

Fag.

Die Prinzessin und der Holzprinz verlassen tanzend die Bühne.
A báb és a királykisasszony kitáncol a színpadról.
The princess and the wooden prince leave, still dancing,the stage,leaving the

Den Prinzen erfaßt die höchste Verzweiflung.
A királyfi végleg kétségbeesik.
prince behind in greatest despair.

Und auf ihr Zauberwort werden alle Dinge lebendig und ziehen im Huldigungstanz vor den Prinzen;
És szavára a dolgok megelevenednek és hódolva a királyfi elé vonulnak.
At her command all things around her are enlivened and now, in rendering homage to the prince, dance before him.

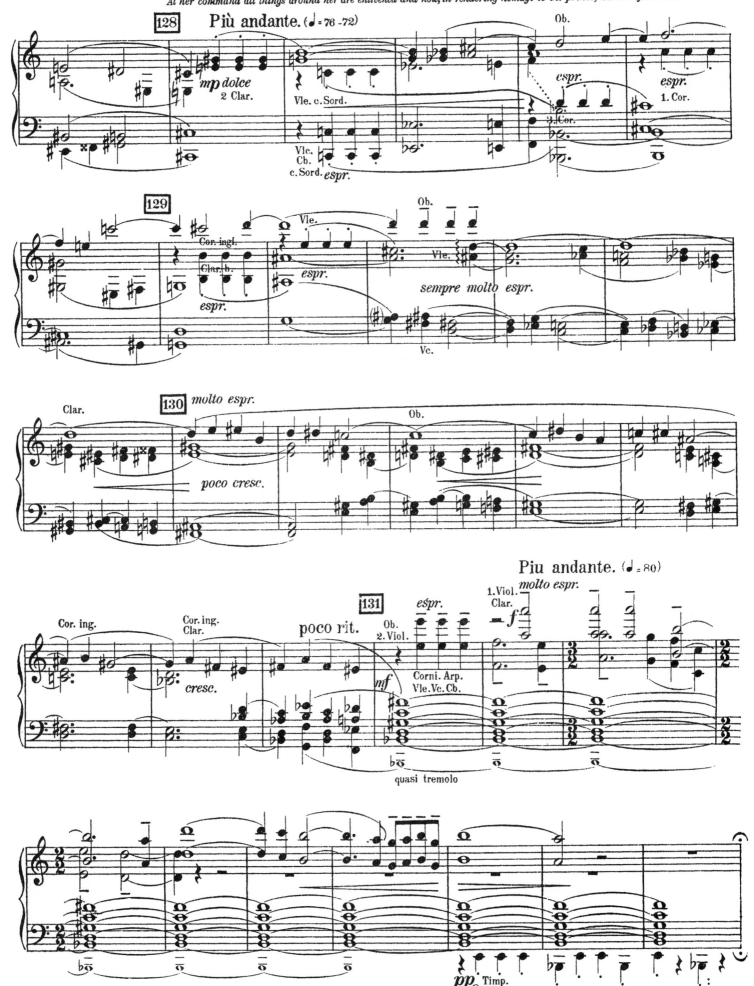

Aus dem Kelch einer großen Blume nimmt die Fee gelocktes Goldhaar und legt es auf den Kopf des Prinzen,
A tündér egy virágnak kelyhéből aranyhajat vesz elő és a királyfi fejére simitja,
Out of the calyx of a big flower the fairy takes curly golden hair and puts it on the prince's head,

aus einer anderen eine Krone und setzt sie ihm auf,
egy másikból koronát és a királyfi fejére teszi,
from another flower she takes a crown with which she adorns his head,

54

aus einer dritten einen Blumenmantel, den sie ihm umlegt.
egy harmadikból palástot és a királyfira adja.
from a third flower she takes a cloak of flowers which she lays round his shoulders.

Große Apotheose. Huldigung der Bäume, der Gewässer und Blumen.
Nagy apoteózis. Sorfalat állnak a fák, vizek, virágok.
Great apotheosis. Homage of the trees, waters and flowers.

Die Fee faßt den Prinzen bei der Hand
A tündér kézenfogja a királyfit *és*
The fairy takes the prince's hand and

und führt ihn nach links bis zum Fuße des Hügels.
átvezeti balra a domb lábához.
leads him to the hill.

Triumph, Pracht und Glanz: „Hier bist du König über alle Dinge."
Diadal, pompa, fényesség: „Ime, itt király vagy."
Triumph, radiancy and splendour. "Here you will be King over everything!"

55

Auf einmal erscheint auf der entgegengesetzten Sei-
Egyszerre csak megjelenik a tulsó oldalon, a szín-
All of a sudden the princess appears on the opposite side

te die Prinzessin mit dem Holzprinzen. Der hat sich schon alle Glieder verrenkt: Perücke, Krone und Mantel hängen ganz schief an ihm.
pad jobb sarkában a királykisasszony a fabábbal; az istenadta már nagyon kificamodott. Koronája félrecsapva, palástja félvállon fityeg,
with the wooden prince. Everything on the wooden prince, wig, cloak and crown, is in disorderly state.

parókája nyakába csúszott.

V. Tanz. *Die Prinzessin zerrt und zupft an ihm und will ihn zum Tanze nötigen.*
V. tánc. *A királykisasszony táncra nógatja a fabábot.*
V. Dance. *The princess in her endeavour to make him dance, pulls and pushes the wooden prince about.*

58

Allegretto. (♩ = 84.)

VI. Tanz. Mit verführerischem Tanze will sie ihn zu sich locken.
VI. Tánc. Magát kelletö tánccal hivogatja magához.
VI. Dance. With her most fascinating smiles the princess tries to persuade the prince to her side to dance with her.

60

VII Tanz. *Die Prinzessin will erschrocken zu ihm eilen, doch der Wald hält sie auf.*
VII Tánc. *A királykisasszony ijedten a királyfi után akar menni, de az ujra megelevenedett erdő nem engedi át.*
VII. Dance. *Quite alarmed the princess hurries forward to him, yet the forest keeps her from him.*

Moderato. (♩ = 69)

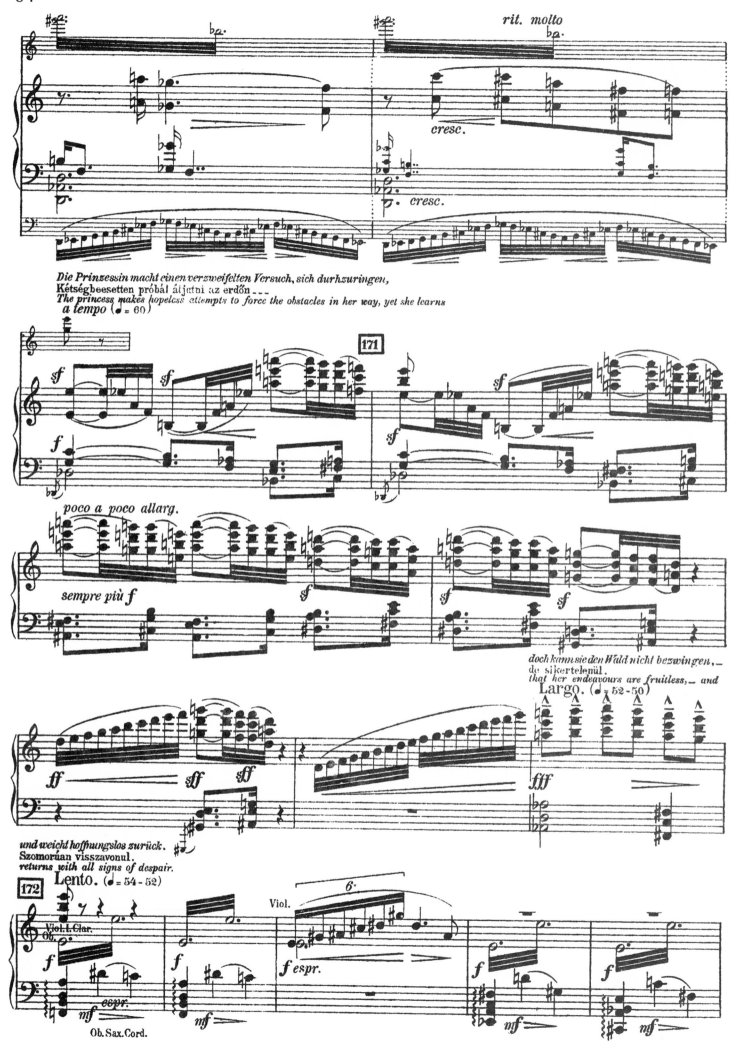

*)*NB. Falls die Darstellung auf der Bühne eine Kürzung erfordert, können hier 10 Takte zwischen A – B und 18 Takte zwischen C – D ausgelassen werden.

*)*NB. Tíz ütem A és B között, tizennyolc C és D között elhagyható, ha a szinpadi játék ezt megkivánja.

*)*NB. If the stage arrangements require a cut to be made the 10 bars from A to B and the 18 bars from C to D may be omitted.

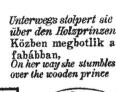

Unterwegs stolpert sie über den Holzprinzen
Közben megbotlik a fabábban,
On her way she stumbles over the wooden prince

und versetzt ihm einen ärgerlichen Fußtritt.
dühösen rug egyet rajta.
and in her anger kicks him.

In ihrer Verzweiflung wirft sie ihre Krone und ihren Mantel weg; schließlich schneidet
Kétségbeesésében ledobja koronáját, palástját; végül még haját is levágja. Aztán szo-
In her utter despair she throws crown and cloak from her, finally cutting her hair off.Then

sie sich sogar das Haar ab; dann kauert sie sich nieder und verbirgt das Gesicht in den Händen.
morúan lekuporodik és kezébe temeti arcát.
she sits down, burying her face in her hands.

Während dessen kommt der Prinz nach vorne.
Közben azonban elésompolyodik a királyfi.
Meanwhile the prince has come in the foreground.

Er erblickt die trauernde Prinzessin, geht zu ihr
Meglátja a bánkódó királykisasszonyt, hozzámegy
Seeing the princess in pain, he goes up to her

und will sie an sich ziehen.
és magához akarja ölelni.
and tries to console her.

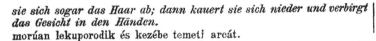

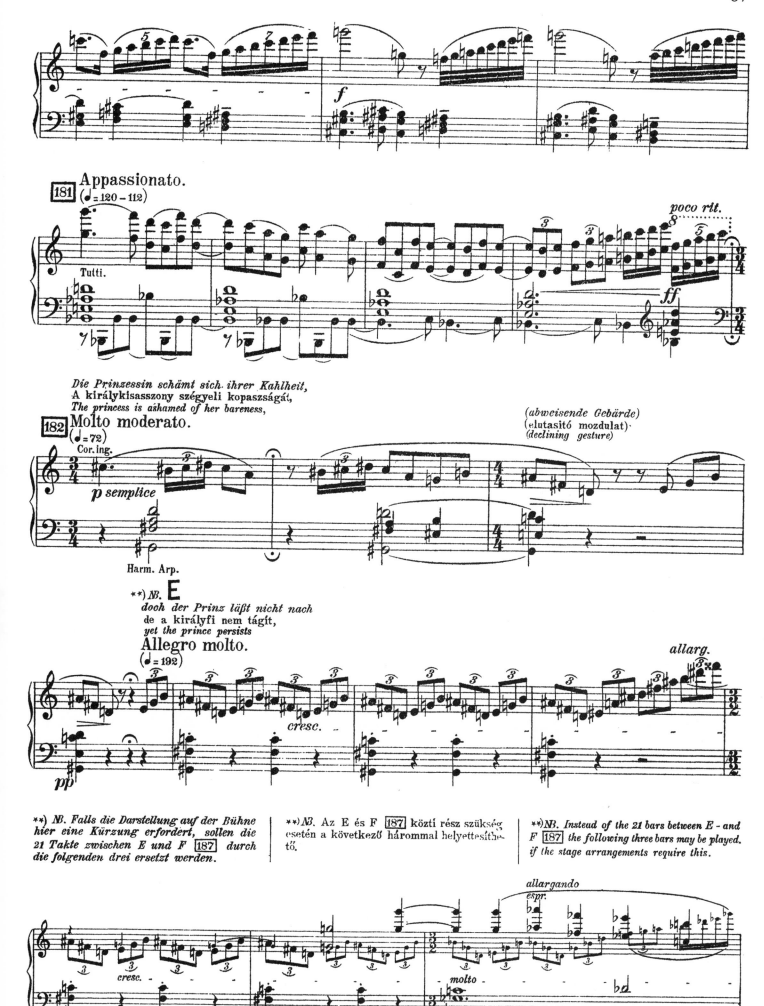

Appassionato.
181 ($\bullet$ = 120 – 112)

Tutti.

poco rit.

ff

Die Prinzessin schämt sich ihrer Kahlheit,
A királykisasszony szégyeli kopaszságát,
The princess is ashamed of her bareness,

182 **Molto moderato.**
($\bullet$ = 72)
Cor. ing.

p semplice

Harm. Arp.

(abweisende Gebärde)
(elutasító mozdulat)
(declining gesture)

) NB. **E
doch der Prinz läßt nicht nach
de a királyfi nem tágit,
yet the prince persists

Allegro molto.
($\bullet$ = 192)

allarg.

cresc.

pp

**) NB. Falls die Darstellung auf der Bühne hier eine Kürzung erfordert, sollen die 21 Takte zwischen E und F 187 durch die folgenden drei ersetzt werden.

**)NB. Az E és F 187 közti rész szükség esetén a következő hárommal helyettesíthető.

**)NB. Instead of the 21 bars between E - and F 187 the following three bars may be played. if the stage arrangements require this.

allargando
espr.

cresc.

molto

68